As God Is by My Side

Chantelle Carlina Stephens

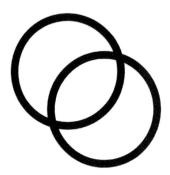

Dreaming Big Together
PUBLISHING

Copyright ©2022 Chantelle Carlina Stephens

All rights reserved.

Book Cover Designed by: Lotus Tree Productions

ISBN: **978-1-913310-75-2**

DEDICATION

To my boys Jayden and Shaqeal I love you both with all my heart, you both make me proud every day! Reach for the stars as the world is yours to become whatever it is that you want to be. Never give up on your hopes and dreams. In loving memory of my first son Elijah born sleeping on 1st December 2005 you will forever be in my heart.

♡

CHANTELLE CARLINA STEPHENS

CONTENTS

"Thy word is a lamp unto my feet and a light unto my path" Psalm 119:105

"God is the joy and the strength of my life He moves all pain, misery and strife, he promise to keep me never to leave me, never ever fallen short of his word I'm gonna fast and praise stay in his narrow way, and keep my life clean every day, I want to go with him when he comes back, I've come to far and I'd never turn back"

John Cleveland

ACKNOWLEDGMENTS

Giving God thanks because without him nothing is possible, he knew me before I had entered my mother's womb. He gave me life, so I owe him my all. To my Ny thank you for being there for us, love you. Shout out to my mom and dad, brothers and sisters like branches on a tree we all have our own different directions in life but with the one grounded root we will always remain the same, love to you all. A big shout out to Rev Dr Trevor Adams who introduced me to Sabrina Ben Salmi who made it possible for this book to come to life and I would like to also thank Lashai Ben Salmi for designing my book cover. To those friends who were in my life for a short amount of time it was a lesson learnt, I thank you. The untimely passing of my cousin Teval aka Big T who was taken by covid19 in 2021. Gone too soon, you will be forever in our hearts and never far from our thoughts ♡

TROUBLED TEEN

To be leaving year 6 at St George's primary school and getting ready to be a part of secondary school life was so exciting for me, more importantly so that my best friend Teresa would be joining me along with a few others from our class. I remember the last day, saying our goodbyes it was quite emotional because I knew I would miss my teacher Mrs. Kendall and all my friends who were off to different secondary schools.

The first few days of secondary school was quite a different experience to primary school. Holte secondary school in Lozells was huge, like a maze. I made a few friends but stayed with my bestie and the few others who were from my primary school. I did also have my big brother Delroy but he wasn't the 'look out for little sis' kind of brother, I would see him around the school but he just did is own thing where I was concerned.

I'd say a few months in, things were going pretty well, I enjoyed all of my lessons apart from the ones I found boring which were math, geography and sometimes science and I had managed to know my way around the school without having to ask anyone for directions. I remember one day walking down a corridor on my way to lesson when one girl called Ruth who was in year 9 at the time had targeted me, she never touched me but always would corner me with her friends and just say hurtful things to me, that I was ugly, that I smelt, which probably was a fact as at this time I used to bed wet. Not sure why, I remember my mom taking me to doctors and clinic appointments. I remember trying the bed wetting alarm but didn't find it very helpful but last resort was the medication that seemed to work for me from time to time.

Walking around the school whenever the bell would go left me in a bag of nerves from fear of bumping into the year 9 bully Ruth and her click, now as an adult looking back on little scared 12-year-old me in year 7 I do believe I had really bad anxiety, at the time I didn't know why I would feel so scared, emotional and overtime depressed. I remember walking home from school one time in tears and stopped by at a phone box which was at the top of the road that I lived on to call ChildLine. I stayed in that phone box for about half an hour just pouring my heart out to this nice lady on the other end of the line telling her about everything and how I felt, she had suggested I tell my parents what was happening.

When I got home, I had told my mom about what was happening in school, and she did what any mother would do and reported it to the school but that just made matters worse where the vile taunts comments and being laughed at by Ruth and her click just got worse and became more threatening. One thing though she never touched me but made me feel ever so scared and nauseous, I always think maybe if I had spoken back and defended myself maybe this would have stopped? but instead it continued, and I had then left to join my younger sister at perry common secondary school.

This was a new venture for me, huge school. I had recognized a couple of girls that were in my class from St Georges, so I didn't feel so alone in my now year 8 going onto year 9. I made a few friends, so I felt quite comfortable in the first year. Enjoyed all the same subjects apart from math, I never really put my all into math although I understand basic math but when it gets more difficult and complicated, I would tend to switch off and focus on something else, like my math teacher Mr. Ellis with the curly eyebrows, I would stare at them for ages wondering how on earth they twirl up like that. So, at times out of boredom I would twirl the end of my eyebrow, don't ask me why I did that, not such a good idea as now my eyebrow has a little twirl at the end, hope it don't grow out of control like my old math's teacher's huge twirl of an eyebrow.

Eventually the bullying had started again at this school by a girl with the same name as me but spelt differently. She too like Ruth and her click would target me amongst others.

I always wondered is it because I'm quiet and keep myself to myself I come across as an easy target for bullies? Like her too she never touched me but would always comment and say something to make her click look and laugh at me like some class clown. She had got my best friend to slap me in the face, which ended up with us physically fighting, I remember it had taken three teachers to get me off her, I'd never felt so much anger and rage in my life but had got excluded from the school for the one time I had stood up for myself. During my teens I do have a few fond memories such as dressing up my little sister Jamilla and getting her to strike a pose for the camera, one pose I remember was getting her to sit facing forward with one of them old school brick Motorola phones and snap. I would also be the one behind the camcorder capturing family gatherings. A lot of times I'd just be in my own world and love my own company, I remember walking through town once and someone stopped me and said "smile! It may never happen' there I am forcing a smile and replying with my cheesiest grin, "this is my natural resting face! 'I'm good'. Over the years I came to find out this natural face was just 'the Stephens look' not me pulling no screw face.

RUNAWAY

My mum had got me an educational social worker her name was Jeane, I would never forget her she was such a great support. After much consideration I had thought maybe I should give Holte a try again, after all I did have a few friends at the school who I had missed, and Ruth and her click would have been long gone. Well, that was a bad decision as I was targeted by students in my year group upon my return, it's like they all knew the reason why I had left in the first place, I became public enemy number one in my year, unsure why? but I know it made me feel ever so horrible inside, I would cry myself to sleep at night in fear of school the next day. I remember being targeted by a bunch of girls in my year I didn't even know, so I guess they had started the school whilst I was at perry common.

I do believe it's true the saying be careful with your words as it can cut like a sword. I remember being in PE being called fat, or the song taunts big, fat and heavy. This just got worse as the days went by and I just couldn't take anymore. Day's when I would skip school, I would visit Brandwood end cemetery where my granddad John Stephens is buried. I would just sit on the grass and reminisce on the short but great memories I have of my granddad. I remember when I must have been about 4 or 5, he would scare me by making his false teeth come out of his mouth, I'd be traumatized but he would find it hilarious. I would always go back and ask him to do it again, I also remember him taking me to the park, pushing me on a swing and buying me mars bar. His death in 1988 had left me heartbroken, I wasn't able to say goodbye at the funeral because my dad thought I was too young, I was 5 when he had passed so I could understand my dad's choice on that one.

I remember I would always watch his funeral on video tape in tears because I loved him so much, it was a bond that I cherished more than any other family relationship. The bullying continued to take its toll on me, it was a downward spiral into depression and my only comfort was food. Which is why I had gained the weight. I still to this day struggle with the weight and it is a sensitive subject for me, it has always been a barrier and something I have struggled with, easy to put on but hard to get rid of. One summer evening I had come home from school and decided I couldn't carry on with life anymore. I just felt like I had no one to turn to and felt empty and sad and scared inside, so I took a load of pills and tried to take my life. I remember waking up in hospital and having to drink this thick black stuff and spent the night in hospital for observation.

The next morning a social worker had asked me why I did what I had did, I had told her I keep getting bullied in school and that I was unhappy with my life. I never returned back to Holte but Jean had thought best I try Handworth wood girls which was the worst of them all. I remember bringing a camcorder into the school just to show badly misbehaved and vile these girls were, one in particular who bulled me called Natalie, cornered me in front of a group of girls asking me questions of a sexual nature. As all the girls surrounded me and called me a virgin and laughed in my face, I felt please God just help me through this I can't take it anymore. My older brother Errol on my dad's side had helped me through this, when I had told him he soon came to my rescue and would not stop till we found her, and he had warned her off me and that was the end of that. Never did I return to that school again.

I did go to an alternative provision where I had finished my schooling years at a place called the link Centre which I absolutely loved! at this school I had made new friends, enjoyed all my lessons even the boring ones, we even had a weekend away at a cottage in Wales, the views were breath taking. During secondary school life I did wonder, why was this happening to me? why do I get targeted every time? I did try the Muslim faith for less than a week as my dad had totally forbidden this in our home. At home I never really felt happy during these troubled times I would always be running away from home to my nans (dad's mom), I do miss her, she was my go-to place whenever I felt down upset, lost and stressed. I do remember one time during my runaway teen years I had found solace with the Brooks family. They are a huge family in Stafford, and we would visit their church from time to time.

I remember the church on Sandon Road, Stafford is a beautiful place. At this church I was given my own room which was based right at the top of the church, I kind of felt like Quasimodo from the hunchback of Notre Dame, but not in a bad way, I was treated like part of the family, it was great I loved it. I remember decorating my room, putting my stamp on the place with my GCSE artwork of a dolphin I had drawn, pinned up on my wall centre of place because I have always had a love for dolphins. I also had drawn a side-by-side picture of a woman half elderly and half young with a load of different styled clocks in the background to represent time.

Two of my proud pieces of artwork but had only been unfairly graded a D for all of my effort. Though my life in Stafford was blissful, peaceful and bright there was something missing. I was missing home really bad, Birmingham, my family so I decided to head back home.

DJ VIP

524 Centre Stratford Road, Birmingham also known at the time as South Birmingham College was where I studied Media Production Level 3. I absolutely loved the fact that I had the opportunity to study what I had a love for which was media, my dream job has always been to work backstage at the MOBO (Music of Black Orientation) Awards. I never did get to the MOBO's even after reaching out to them a number of times. 524 Centre was where I had my first opportunity at DJ'ing across the airwaves on the college community radio station. I loved it! I do think it's in the bloodstream because as a kid I remember when my dad also known as Mikey Studio at the time would DJ on a well-known Birmingham station called PCRL. He would play his lovers rock music across the airwaves and also play out and clash against other local DJ's. At the time I couldn't stand my dad's kind of music but since becoming older and understanding the music I love it.

I am particularly a fan of Sandra Cross and her music, especially country living, and I adore you are my two top favourites of hers. In college I went by the DJ name VIP (Very Important Princess) and would play my favourite music at the time which was R&B, hip hop, a little dancehall and a slice of garage. Here is where I met my friend Mista Smoove who would always be a laugh at college and I was amazed at his love for R&B music and how he would always know the latest tunes, just watching him in front of the console and the microphone was like magic, this came naturally to him. Whilst at college I had the opportunity to play on a local radio station called Premier fm. This was just amazing; I was so excited! Having the opportunity to do what I love, just talking across the airwaves and playing my favourite music was such a great feeling. I remember one time having the opportunity to interview girl band Monroe who had just burst onto the scene with their new cover of 'smile'.

Talk about star struck, after interviewing the girls they had given me a signed a4 poster with all of their autographs on it, wow I was on cloud nine. Another star struck moment was when my sister Tamira and I had the opportunity to meet R&B boy band Damage, who were on Galaxy radio station at the time, we knew they were on the radio, so we just waited outside until they came out and not only had a picture with them all but had a walk and a talk with them down broad street, talk about an epic moment! We loved every moment.

During my time at college and DJ'ing on Premier radio I was offered the opportunity to go to South Africa on an educational visit for a week. I wasn't working at the time so had told one of my tutors I was unable to afford the trip, I was then totally gob smacked when I was told the fee is covered as long as your able to come and be a part of it.

I was in total shock, beyond belief and truly blessed to be given such an amazing opportunity. My trip to South Africa was definitely an eye opener that I would never forget. The apartheid museum that I had visited had broken my heart, left me moved inside with emotions, I just couldn't hold in the tears seeing and learning of such torture that our ancestors of Africa had endured during those times, this is the pain of our history Black history runs deep. Whilst in South Africa we had gone on an amazing South African Safari in the National Kruger Park and had also visited a small village to see what life was like for the local village people. They took us into their homes, they showed us how they made their cultural dishes and how they played music on the drums and of cause the awesome dance moves. I remember one night relaxing up in what seemed like a tent, I was resting as I was suffering with really bad menstrual cramps, something I have suffered with ever since it had first started when

I was 17. As I woke from my little nap in this tent it was very quiet, not sure where everyone else was but I heard what sounded like a growl, I was scared to come out in case it was a lion wanting to eat me so I decided to stay where I was until my fellow college team had returned, I don't think I've held in a toilet break for so long before think I would have exploded if I had to hold it any longer. We had also drove past the house of the late Winnie Mandela which was another star struck moment in my life.

I will never forget my trip to South Africa because it was a mixture of emotions while there, beautiful place, breath taking views, the scenery was just captivating and even had the opportunity to visit a local radio station there too. All this was captured on camera, till this day I have not had the opportunity to watch any of it back as it belongs to the college. I have over the years reached out to the college to see if the footage is anywhere to be found but sadly not had any joy with that. If it was down to me, I would have been editing that footage from the get-go as I love editing video footage.

CHANTASTIC TO THE WORLD

There are many holiday destinations I would love to visit such as Dominica, Antigua, the Bahamas and back to the motherland Africa. I would particularly love to take my boys to visit Gambia and go on the Juffure Roots tourist trail. I do eventually at some point want to visit our family roots in Somaliland where my granddad was born and meet my mom's side of the family. I think it's important that my boys know about our black history roots and to also appreciate the little things in life that a lot take for granted. I never did get the chance to meet my granddad (mom's dad), my mom only has the one picture of him holding her up as a baby. I do remember my mom telling me about him being a fisherman in Middlesbrough back in the 60s and the stories my nan used to tell me about when she was with him, he was her true love and would say he wasn't your typical Somali as he loved a game of dominoes with his fellow workers when they would meet up at a cafe called the boarder.

I still to this day would love to visit Middlesbrough just to see where my granddad once lived, but as my nan has now passed on, we only have the information that was given to us at the time. I was intrigued to find out more about the Somali side of my family which I knew only a little about, but always did wonder if my grandad was alive and I had turned into an investigator to try and find out if he was still living. So, I started asking around to see if anyone knew of my grandad Muhammed Dirie also known as Yahye.

As I wasn't getting very far with my investigations, I had thought it was time for a career move. I had seen a job fair for camp America and thought I'd love to try it out. The film troop Beverly Hills had sprung to mind, an old childhood favourite movie of mine alongside she's out of control another old school favourite and adventures in baby-sitting there are so many favourites the list goes on. So, I had gone along to this job fair, and I was spoilt for choice, the amount of different summer camp employers looking for camp counsellors was too much for me to choose from, how could I choose? I had gone along to a few of the employers who were offering work but the one that stood out for me was Camp Catksill which is located in a little town called Liberty.

The interview went well, and I was hired on the spot, just like that. Camp Catskill are a special needs summer camp, now I had never worked in this field of work before but felt drawn to sign up for this camp, so I did. Thanks to my parents they had paid the fee for me to go, and all I needed to do was get packed and ready to start my summer job. June 2001 I was so nervous but excited to be given such an amazing opportunity to work stateside the big US of A! A place I've only ever dreamed of going to and now it's happening, I get to stay in New York for three months, overly excited.

Once I had got to camp, I had set up in cabin 6, no privacy but it was great, we even decorated the outside of our cabin with clouds a little sunshine and the number 6. Once I was settled it felt more like a study boot camp which I must say dragged. It was two weeks of lectures which all camp counsellors had to participate in. We went over rules and regulations, health and safety, dos and don'ts, medications, safeguarding and whistle blowing. My brain was sizzled by the time first lectures were done. Once the campers arrived, we were all assigned with our campers by our camp leader. My first camper was quite challenging, she literally kept me on my toes that first week.

She was great to work with and we had fun taking part in all of the different activities.

After the first month I started to become homesick and was missing my family, I remember walking down to the den where there was one phone box, I had to wait a while before I could make a call to my family. When I did finally get to use the phone, I would be excited to tell my family about the hard challenging but yet rewarding work it was to be a camp counsellor, by the time my call was seconds from ending I'd feel my eyes filling up, but then would dust myself off and get back to it.

The good thing about the camp life was when your two weeks work were finished, you would be able to opt in to help take the campers back to New York City on the coach and whilst there you'd be able to enjoy your weekend before heading back to camp with new campers. I remember booking my weekend off with a friend I had made called Sue-Young. She and I had booked our weekend off to have a tour around NYC times square, it was great. Another great weekend I remember a few of the cabin 6 camp counsellors did a spice girls tribute and of course I had to play the top role of being scary spice and Sue-Young wanted to be posh spice. What a great night that was! ha-ha.

We had a great laugh and a lot of fun times together; I remember making a great friend called ChiChi short for Chilufya. She was from Zambia, she was my go-to and would always give the best advice and would always be seen making extra dollar because everyone on camp wanted their hair done, it's amazing because all these counsellors were from all over the world and working together building great friendships. Sadly, ChiChi and I lost contact after camp. When camp had come to an end in August 2001 I felt a sense of sadness, this had been my home away from home for the past three months, the friendships I had made I would miss most. The experiences I would never forget as this had opened the door for my career in support work.

I was hoping to stay on in 'The Big Apple', but I had run out of funds so had to head back home. A month after I had got to the UK it broke my heart to hear of the tragic terrorism attack on the world trade centre, a day the world was mourning with America such a sad tragedy. Late 2001 I remember getting a call from a guy called Muahmmed telling me he had news about my mom's family. This was such great news to hear!! I remember screaming and my mom wondering what on earth got me to scream in such a way, I remember telling her we had to go to Stratford Road in Sparkbrook which is a UK version of Somaliland. Once we got there my mom and I we're so excited just to hear what great news was about to come. The news about my grandad not living was the heart-breaking truth, we were told he had passed away in 1974 somewhere in Dubai.

I would love to find out where his final resting place is. My mom had found out she has a huge family in Hargeisa and that they did know of my mom because my grandad spoke of her many times when he was back home. This news was bittersweet. The following year my mom flew out to Somaliland to meet her sister and long-lost family for the first time.

FAMILY BAPTISM

I remember my mom cleaning at the old Matthew Bolton college before it got knocked down when she had met her friend Pet.

Pet had invited my mom and the rest of our family to a church in King's Norton at the co-op Hall (the upper room) above some shops. I remember visiting the church for the first time, the bredrin were warm and welcoming and I remember pastor Johnson with his glasses, his posh suit and how he would play his guitar. The kind of rhythm he would string would go with any Pentecostal hymnal. I'd been to church before, but this one had something special about it that made me want to stay and learn more. It became my second home and I enjoyed learning about God, I loved the fellowship and worship. When I would be in service whether it be during the word being read or the worship and praise, I would be moved on the inside, something in my heart would move me. The song says the Holy ghost power is moving just like a magnet and I believe this strongly. I felt like all that time during my troubled teen years that this was it, this was the place I needed to be at to fill that void of emptiness.

This church was it for me, the upper room Pentecostal Apostolic Church. I remember my first time to experience the church convocation at the upper room, talk about a power House! Good lord! Once that praise and worship had started, I would see people jumping, dancing, running skipping waving and all sorts without a care in the world, this I learnt was God the power of his holy spirit touching the people who reach out to him. I would watch in amazement like wow!! This is incredible I want this. So, we continued at this church and understanding the teachings of baptism in Jesus name as it clearly states in the bible. Acts 2 verse 38 says 'Then Peter said unto them, repent and be baptized every one of you in the name of Jesus Christ for the remission of sins and ye shall receive the gift of the Holy ghost' there it is in black and white it gives us clear instruction of what we had to do.

Now bearing in mind it also states in the bible that Jesus said in Matthew 28:19 'Go ye therefore, and teach all nations, baptizing them in the name of the Father, and of the Son, and of the Holy Ghost' It baffles me why there is so much conflict with churches about this, as Jesus specifically said to teach all nations to baptize in the name of? So, what is that name? It is the name of Jesus. He didn't say to baptize into the titles. Father, son and Holy ghost are titles, aren't they? Not names. The titles will not give removal of sin but by the name of JESUS Christ we shall be saved amen. So that time came where we as a family had got together with our pastor Johnson and agreed that we would all like to be water baptized in Jesus name.

We had the talk that once we are baptized, we are a new creation, things we used to do we should do them no more, old ways would need to be gone and to live a Christ like life. To seek heaven as our eternity home and to live for Christ, without him nothing is possible. So, we had all agreed that this is what we all wanted to do. In 1999 Mom, dad and nan (on my mom's side) myself and my sisters all decided to take on Jesus name in water baptism. I remember for myself this was such a surreal moment, I was dressed in all white, white headscarf, white gown, I felt like an angel. I felt mixed emotions like my heart was racing I put that down to my nerves, I felt an overwhelming sense of emotions going through me like adrenaline.

As I slowly went down into the warm pool, I had repeated the words I was asked to say about making God my Lord and saviour and the reason why I am getting baptized, from what I remember I had said so I can build a closer relationship with God, next thing I was pushed under water then lifted up with a warm overflowing feeling of joy in my heart that filled my eyes with tears

This new journey of salvation I had embarked on with our Lord and Saviour Jesus Christ was great. I was enjoying going to church and learning more, also visiting other fellow sister churches. I felt like I was growing a close relationship with God. My top Gospel play list on my mp3 player included songs by Carlene Davis at your feet, Sanchez Amazing grace and my number one go to song by Mary Mary called 'Can't give Up Now' every time I would play this song it would pull on my heart strings and would uplift my spirit. I never got filled with the spirit or spoke in a heavenly language, but I have come ever so close to it, I've felt an overwhelming sense of love like a volt of electricity running through my veins but felt so good that my body would quicken, what an amazing experience.

I do believe if I would just leap out on faith and forget about who's around me watching me, I do believe that feeling would have taken me to a whole new experience with being filled with the spirit, but I always held back out of fear of who was watching me, I have never been one to stand out in the crowd and be centre of attention, I'd be the one hiding away in the background. As my relationship started to grow with God the enemy was on the prowl, so there would be times I would yearn to go to church but the enemy would see to it that I would be unable to go.

Missing church would make me so sad as I felt like church was my second home. As I couldn't get to go as much as I wanted, I became less interested and started to disconnect from church they call it 'backslide'. I remember when I did get to go back to church there were a few newbies, I remember a group of girls that were new in the upper room who had reminded me of the bullies from school, there was a heated exchange of words between the girls and I and from that I never returned back to church.

BACKSLIDE

Me, my sister Tam and our friend at the time SB would be up London at least once a fortnight clubbing. We would book our tickets from Moor Street train station to travel to London as it seemed the cheaper option to go from this station. Once in London we would be getting ready for the night sipping on the strongest beers at the time which was super tenants' cringe! but it was super tee to us. Box of ciggies to go with the alcohol or if money was tight, it would be a box of tobacco for role ups. We would love the Somali raves and was welcomed by the Somali community as they were aware of our mix and were amazed by us as no one had ever heard of such a mix, so we stood out from the crowd. My mom is half Somali and half white and my dad's parents were from JA but my dad was born here.

I would personally call it the VIP mix. Proud to be quarter Somali quarter white and half Jamaican. I remember one weekend up in London I was asked to DJ at a club called the EQ arena in Hackney Wick. The area looked like some run down back street in the middle of nowhere. I said yes, I'd do it of course why not, just reminded me of my days on the radio but this time it was in a club with people dancing!! Wowzers!! And no, I wasn't offered money for my services, now looking back on it I should have got paid at least £200 for doing a set, look at the prices DJ's charge nowadays an arm and a leg but I offered my services for free because I was just so excited about playing my favourite play list at the time which included songs like Fat Joe and Ashanti what's luv and Keith Murray Candy bar.

After my set I had joined my sis and friend on the dance floor as we danced the night away till the early hours. As we were all leaving the club, I remember my sister and I were trying to get a ride, as we were waiting a dispute had started outside of the club. The dispute got quite violent and ended up with one of our friends being bottled and knocked out unconscious. Everyone went crazy and scattered like wild animals. I had later found out the friend who was bottled was ok thank God. It was during this time I met Mustafa who was of Somali origin my first love. He wasn't your typical Somali, he had a love for Jamaican food and culture and would even speak patois which left my jaw hitting the floor after hearing him I'd be like how you speak like that? I won't attempt it personally as I was born here, I remember back in the day hearing it from my dad when he was angry but not like this.

I was 19 and Mustafa and I had been dating for about 4 months and it felt like love was in the air, boy was I wrong. I remember when Mustafa and I wanted to spend time together we would meet up at his uncle's flat in Leicester, but he was originally from London. I remember one time travelling to Leicester in pain because of my menstrual cycle, but I was just happy that I'd be in company with my then sweetheart, so I didn't mind travelling in pain as long as I got to be with Mustafa. I remember getting to his uncle's flat and he was quite empathic to my situation. As he lay down with me on the bed, he stroked my head and told me he would be right back, I assumed he probably wanted to get us something to eat from the shop.

"See ya in abit Chan, Chan" he said, he would always call me that and off he went. I had dozed off and woke to being caressed underneath my top, half asleep I pushed his hand away but then I felt a wet kiss on my face and an unfamiliar smell, as I opened my eyes to see it wasn't Mustafa my heart must have jumped out of my throat as I jumped and stood and asked "who are you?? Where's Mustafa??" He replied "it's OK, Mustafa said I can come chill and keep you company, his gone back to London" my heart sank, I couldn't believe It! And was in total shock and I was scared, so I went toilet and locked myself in there for what seemed like an hour. Once I came out, I seen this Somali looking dude conked out flat out on the bed, I grabbed the keys and escaped out of the flat. As my cramps were getting worse, I was outside cold, alone and in pain in the rain just walking to God knows where.

I don't remember much after that; I just remember waking up in a hospital. I didn't wait around to be seen, cramps had stopped so I had got out of there and headed to the train station. Before getting on the train back home I called Mustafa from a phone box and he answered, I asked him where he was, he said he had to go back home. From that call I locked him off blocked and deleted and never spoke or heard from him again.

♡Elijah Jeremiah Adegbuyi♡

Having a positive result on a pregnancy test got me overwhelmed with excitement and joy! I couldn't wait to let my family know that I was expecting my first. My pregnancy went really well, it was a whole new experience for me being a first-time mom. I remember during my pregnancy I had gone to Blackpool pleasure Beach with my partner at the time and his family during the summer holidays. We had both gone on the big one the Pepsi max ride it was called at the time, it was a fun family day out. As time went by my belly got bigger and I remember having interaction with my son at bath times which was his favourite time because he would be doing all sorts as I would watch in amazement at my belly just moving around as I sat there relaxed in the bath, I really loved feeling him move inside and kick, or if he had the hiccups, I would feel it.

Special bonding moments with my baby boy and I. As winter started to draw near, I thought best to start getting things ready, I had his cot set up in my room, I got everything Johnson's baby and pampers new born nappies, only the best for my baby boy. I remember my baby's dad had brought his pushchair and a few other little bits. I remember buying a cute baby Santa outfit with little baby Christmas booties that played a Christmas rhyme when you press the button, so cute. As the days were getting closer the pregnancy was getting heavier, I remember at one point going to the hospital because I had thought I had a show and I was getting cramps, they had sent me home as it was a false alarm. Days went by and one morning I had woken and felt something wasn't right as I didn't feel my baby move.

I went to my mom's house as I was concerned and spoke to her about it, she said babies tend to get lazy in the last days of pregnancy as I've also read. My mom suggested I try to drink some ice-cold water, tried that and still nothing. She suggested I try to move my tum gently with my hands because he may be sleeping, tried that and nothing. At this time, I started to panic and asked my mom if she could take me to the hospital so I could get checked out, she told me she couldn't take me because she was cooking her husband's dinner, so she asked if I would mind her husband taking me.

My mom's husband and I have not had the best relationship, it's literally been rocky ever since my mom got married to this bloke, but she loves him so I would usually just keep my distance whenever he was around for peace sake.

At this moment, even though I dislike this man, I was in no position to dispute him taking me to the hospital I just know I had to get there to get checked out. My mom's husband took me to the hospital, but we didn't speak as we just don't talk in general.

Once I had got to the hospital, the nurse had put the monitor on my tummy and picked up a trace, "ahh there he is" she said, oh my! tears of joy came and a sigh of relief, but that was short lived when I was told that it was my pulse that was picked up not my baby's heartbeat.

I was then taken into a room with a doctor with my mom's husband in tow and the doctor had scanned me on a coloured looking ultrasound scan, moments later I heard the dreaded words that no parent wants to hear "I'm sorry but there is no heartbeat, so sorry for your loss" in that very moment my whole world just came crashing down, I felt the most unbearable heartache I've ever felt in my life, all I could do is scream out in pain and cry uncontrollably, this was torture.

In this moment my mom's husband tried to console me and I screamed at him "get your hands off me!! I want my mom!!" I just couldn't stop crying, I do remember him calling my mom, she was on loudspeaker, I can remember asking her if she can come and be with me, she too was crying on the phone it was all very emotional.

So many things went through my mind once it had started to sink in. How am I going to give birth? Maybe they made a mistake? Where will he sleep? What about his things? My head just went into overdrive I was scared and felt alone. I remember speaking with a doctor on the evening of November 30th asking if I could have a c section, but I was told I had to give birth naturally, the thought of this scared me. On the morning of 1st December my mom, her best friend Tracey and my sis Tamira were all there with me for support. I was given the medication to start off my labour, now all we had to do was wait.

Going through labour was hard! The most unbearable pain I had ever felt, as I had to do this on my own, when a woman is giving birth to a baby that is alive, the baby works alongside the mom to work its way down the birth canal. My son was born at 5:15pm on his estimated due date 1st December 2005 weighing a healthy 8lbs 12oz. Once he was out, I didn't hear no cry, not sure why I was expecting a cry, maybe I was just hoping for a miracle.

At first, I couldn't look at my son, I was scared, but moments later I said pass me my baby boy. He was beautiful, just looked like he was sleeping. The only thing that concerned me was his skin that had peeled off his left cheek. I had asked why has this happened to his skin? I was told that when we're in a bath our fingers crinkle up, my Elijah's skin would have blistered being in the amniotic fluid which explained it. He still looked perfect in my eyes. Once my family and I had our time with my baby boy he was taken.

The staff at the hospital were very supportive to my family and I at Birmingham women's hospital. My little sister Keisha had written me a beautiful poem in memory of Elijah, I just remember reading it and the words moved my soul, my eyes filling up with tears and dropping down onto this beautiful heartfelt poem. I was asked what I would like my baby to wear. I had set aside this cute cream peak-a-boo teddy outfit that was ready for him to wear to leave the hospital. Instead of leaving the hospital with my son,

I had left the hospital with a yellow memorial box with a few sentimental memories of my son Elijah. I remember leaving the hospital and hearing the song 'love is just a game' by the magic numbers playing on the radio, I downloaded the song and kept it on repeat, this was my go-to song at this time. A couple of days after coming out of hospital I got my baby boy Elijah's name tattooed on my back.

21

'In loving memory of Elijah'

I'm so sorry I could not meet you and see your face, But I know you're watching down over us with the Lord amazing Grace, A beautiful baby boy, yes that's what you are, A gift from God like the amazing stars, Now the angels have took you in their loving wings, so you may see the Lord our King, You meant the world to me, although this sad day was meant to be, This is to you, my little sweet nephew, This is to let you know that I will always love you, When loss and sorrow is swept away, Yes, that's when I will see you...that one sweet day. You meant the world to me Elijah...

I love you now and forever *Love auntie Keisha xxxxxxxxx*

This poem was written by my little sister Keisha who was 14 at the time.

BUS STOP ATTRACTION

It was a warm September evening when my sister and I had gone walking down the Bristol Road into town to get some beers, on the way, walking towards us we were stopped in our tracks by a young man who had greeted us with a 'good evening, ladies'. We stopped and started to chat with this young man who had told us his name was Jason. As Jason sat at the bus stop chatting with my sister and I, I had noticed him giving me that side eye. I was shy and would just look away but there was an instant attraction. He had told me he was single and had no kids and I too was single. We headed back to my flat and realized we had so much in common. We clicked, it was an instant chemistry, we would even sing the same church songs and reminisce on our times growing up in church.

I thought to myself I am in luck here! good looking guy, single, has a Christian faith background like me, what more could a girl ask for? we hit it off straight away and became official. Before I knew it, he was living with me in my flat, it was great I was literally on cloud 9.

A few months into our relationship I had become pregnant. Straight away it was mixed emotions, happiness because of being pregnant but also a fear because of what had happened with my first born. I remember when I had found out, I had called Jason on the phone to let him know the news. I couldn't tell if he was happy or not, he just seemed casual about it, so I didn't look too much into it, I just thought maybe his in shock. As my pregnancy went by, Jason wasn't really the supportive type, he never came to any antenatal appointments and to no scans, but my mom was there to support me throughout my pregnancy. I was seen on a weekly basis by my midwife because of what had happened with Elijah.

I did find out the cause of the stillbirth was placenta abruption; this is where the placenta comes away and my blood had mixed with Elijah's. So, this pregnancy I was ever so nervous and took things easy. With this pregnancy my doctor had booked a planned Caesarean because of my stillbirth. So, the date was set for 27th November 2007. I had to be at the Birmingham women's hospital for 8am. I was so excited and nervous at the same time. I would be constantly touching my tum to make sure I could feel my little man kicking. Once at the hospital Jason and I had got ourselves prepared whilst my mom waited for us in the waiting room.

I remember laying down in the operating theatre just looking around thinking wow! today is the day I get to meet my little man, what an overwhelming feeling. Once they had started the procedure, I was happy that they had music playing in the background, I couldn't feel a thing as I had the epidural. All I could feel is my body slightly swaying from side to side as I was lying down on this operating table, it was like having the washing up done but inside of me. A very different experience. As the curtain was up, I couldn't see a thing, but Jason sat by my side and had a peep over the curtain and looked back at me with the widest eyes like he had seen something he shouldn't have? I slightly chuckled.

11:59am and right in the middle of the song rock DJ by Robbie Williams I heard a cry, and I was shown my little healthy baby boy weighing 9lbs 6oz. My little chunky boy was here I couldn't wait to hold him and watched in amazement as Jason held our little boy who was wrapped in a hospital baby blanket. I remember being up on the ward with my little baby Jayden, just before Jason said his goodbyes to us, he told me he would always be there for us and that he wasn't going nowhere, I took this as literate, and those words stayed with me.

I was so thankful to have my healthy baby boy here with me, I just couldn't take my eyes off him. During our night's stay at the hospital, I would wake during the night to give him a feed, wind him till he burped and then off to sleep he went. Thank you, God, for my perfect baby boy, what more could I ask for my world is complete. The next morning, I was discharged from the hospital and my mom came for us in her car to take us home. What a beautiful surprise my flat was blitzed from head to toe, big thanks to Jason and most of all his auntie Janet.

MOTHERHOOD

I was housebound for a couple of weeks after coming home with Jayden because of having such a major operation. I was quite nervous about having my stitches out and I didn't know what to expect when the midwife came. Thankfully it was a piece of cake, and I didn't feel a thing, me worrying over nothing typical me. The midwife was great, she admired my scar and said "Wow! looks like they've done a VB job on ya!" (Victoria Beckham aka Posh Spice) she also weighed Jayden and gave him his checks, and all was fine.

The one thing I struggled with was breastfeeding, I lasted about a week and a half, the excruciating pain was too much for me to bare, but I did try my best, but it would bring me to tears every time I had tried. I had ended up buying the cow & gate formula as I remember my mom giving it to my younger brother and sisters. The best feeling was taking my little Jayden out for the first time in his graco pushchair. I loved it!!I remember stepping out for the first time, neighbours' cooing over my bundle of joy and giving their congratulations it was beautiful I felt overwhelmed with joy and felt truly blessed.

Beginning of 2008 I had another positive pregnancy result, I had to double check just to be sure and yes, I was expecting our second child. Shocked and happy at the same time, I get to do this journey all over again and my little Jayden will be a big brother. Our family was about to expand I was excited and nervous of this journey but felt happy that I had Jason here with me who I loved with all my heart, I remember our song at the time was Alicia Keys no one, I was happy and in love with my little family in our little flat, picture perfect. The future ahead looked bright but as time went by, Jason once again wasn't around for the antenatal clinics or scans my mom was always there with me. My pregnancy was going really well, Jason became distant, and I would hardly see him, he would tell me he was out with his friends.

I became very weary of his distance and strange behaviour; they call it a woman's intuition and say it's never wrong. I strongly believe if you have doubts about a relationship? and you have to question if your partner is loyal, something isn't right so do something about it. I was about 7 months into our second pregnancy when I checked Jason's phone while he was conked out on my settee fast asleep and for once had left his phone unlocked. I had read a text saying I'm pregnant with your daughter and your never here with me, where are you?'

My heart started to race, my breathing became heavier, and I could feel my little man doing summersaults inside my tummy, I guess he could sense my stress levels going up. I broke down and cried As I was in total disbelief that this man who I had loved was not the man I thought he was. After having a good cry, I text the number back asking who is this? and why are you texting my man's phone? to be honest I thought it was some sick joke but nope was I in for the biggest shock of my life. So, she called, and I had answered. It felt like an interrogation as she was questioning me about his family like, how many brothers does he have? how many sisters etc.

I had answered her correctly but then I had asked her how long have you two been seeing each other as I am currently pregnant with our second son. She gasped in disbelief and had told me she was 5 months pregnant with their daughter and that they had been together for years? I had told her when I met Jason September 2006, he had told me he was single, I would never get in-between a relationship I am not no home wrecker. I told her she was welcome to come to my flat and see him for herself as he was fast asleep, she agreed, and I had text her my address and she had made her way to my flat with her mom.

Jason must have overheard us talking on the phone or had a feeling because he had jumped up from that chair like his pants were on fire and ran out of my flat. When she came in with her mom, the first thing she noticed was his underwear drying on the radiator which she had pointed out and burst into tears, I was just in shock, me and this lady both here face to face both pregnant from the same dude! this is only something I've only ever watched on Jerry Springer, but sadly this was a real-life situation, I was lost for words, hurt and felt very alone as I was about to start this single motherhood life. I also found out his real name wasn't Jason. (But I will continue to refer to him as Jason in this book).

MY BOYS & I

During my heartache and coming to terms with recent events, I found a comfort in listening to the Ashanti foolish album or the Mariah Carey charmbraclet album back-to-back. Music can be a great therapy at times, especially when you can relate to the lyrics in the song. So, as the doctors had given me the OK to give birth naturally although 1 year and 1 month before I had a cesarean with Jayden. 30th October at the women's hospital I remember pacing up and down the hospital corridors as I was adamant my son would not be born on Halloween. The labour pains were gradually coming strong and then stopping so that was a good sign that my little man was on his way.

As I was dilating the midwife had intervened by breaking my waters, what an odd feel that was! no pain just a warm trickle of water, but moments later I had felt the pain coming along a lot stronger than before. This was unbearable pain as I cried out for my mom and cursed out while she had held my hand and told me it would soon be over, I remember my little sister Jamilla being in the room too, telling me to breathe and prompting me like a true supporter saying, "come on Chant you are so brave!" bless her, she must have only been about 14 at the time. I remember whilst in pain and shouting out the midwife in the room was ever so inconsiderate and rude, she actually said to me "tap yuh noise" in her patois accent, what a horrible experience but my mom soon put her in her place because my mom is the no nonsense taking kind of lady. You dare to cross my mom you would soon feel her wrath and she don't hold back either.

11:30pm that final push and the pain was over! I remember as soon as Shaqeal graced the world with his presence the look on Jamilla's face was a picture as she covered her face and turned around, I guess there was just too much afterbirth that made her feel quite nauseous, and just like that and my little bundle of joy Shaqeal was here weighing a healthy 7lbs 12oz. Once back home it was time to figure out how to balance being a single mommy and to figure my routine for my now 11-month-old toddler and my newborn. In the beginning it was hard and quite a challenge, and thought how am I going to do this? I was scared but with God by my side I did it and enjoyed the single life with my two true blessings. Living in my one-bedroom flat was overly crowded with my two boys and I in the one room, thankfully about a month after Shaq was born, I was offered a 3-bedroom house with a garden. God is good, all the time.

Pushing my two boys around in the double pushchair a lot of the time my boys would be mistaken for twins as they both got that twin thing going on even to this day. My two boys have been such a blessing to my life I just can't imagine my life without them, I will never understand how a parent can willingly walk out of their child's life and not be an active parent.

As my boys started nursery, they both loved it, I remember our first residential trip with the nursery, it was a weekend away to Dodford farm where my boys got to enjoy the beauty of nature, horse riding, feeding animals and just to be outdoors and admire God's beauty, we luckily had a huge bedroom to ourselves. We still reminisce and talk about our trip at Dodford farm from time to time. Once my boys started primary school, they had enjoyed the new friendships formed and coming home as proud as ever to show me the hard work that they had both completed in school. As my boys were getting older, they were missing that father figure who was MIA to their lives. Jayden more so would come to me crying asking about his dad, "when can I see dad? can we go to dad's house?" It broke my heart to see my son like this because I could never give him an answer to his heart wrenching questions.

Although Jason would come and see my boys whenever he felt like it, it was never when my boys wanted to see him, this was something that was never consistent which consistency is something that my boys needed from him which was sadly never given. Over the years as my boys have now grown into young men they know where they stand when it comes to the relationship with their father.

Lil me

Dad & mom

My one & only tatt

Magic family pic

Camp Catskill Spice Girls tribute

Jamaica 2016

BLESSED LIFE

My most empowering moment as a single mom of two boys I must say is when I took my boys to Spain in the summer of 2014. It was our first family holiday off on a plane to another country to visit the holiday village in sunny Tenerife, I did feel nervous as I was a single parent with two boys, but I thought why not, big up to all the single mom's and the single dads who would go above and beyond for their kids. I did that! and so can you!! we had the most amazing time in Tenerife. Two years later I decided to push the boat out a bit further and take my boys to the one place I've only ever dreamed of going to and that was Jamaica. Summer of 2016 my boys and I had an all-inclusive two weeks holidays at the holiday inn SunSpree in Mo'Bay. We had the most amazing time out there, absolutely breath taking.

I remember at one point my little Shaq in his bright yellow SpongeBob shorts being pulled centre stage where he did a freestyle and aced the Michael Jackson moonwalk, the crowd went wild! I'm screaming and jumping around like a proud mommy and almost fall flat on my behind. Another treasured memory in JA was at the dolphin cove. Not even just coming face to face but kissing a dolphin! up close and personal, my God talk about a dream come true, my boys and I loved the dolphin encounter, Jayden particularly was a fan of the nighttime entertainment as you would see him up out of his seat dancing away, especially to the lion king show they had put on, that was amazing we loved and cherished every moment.

The moment my boys decided to give their lives to Jesus was a moment I would never forget, I remember both of my boys telling me that this is something that they wanted to do, so 6th November 2016 my boys were baptized in Jesus name at the church of Jesus Christ Apostolic in Sheffield, watching my boys both take the big dip left me in total amazement! How they made such a big decision at their ages I would never forget it, it literally brought tears to my eyes to see this, God is good all the time.

As my boys have grown older, they have matured into young men and make me proud every day. Shaqeal has been a part of a Michael Ellis movie production called 'Boys in the woods' this was his first major role in a mini-YouTube movie. We all have been a part of an Anton Inwood movie production called 'Magnanimous' which is a movie in relation to raising awareness for knife crime, this movie is still yet to be released, hopefully at some point in the near future. My boys have both took part in a breast cancer awareness tribute music video in memory of their late auntie Denise who had sadly passed away on Shaqeal's 10th birthday from breast cancer, the tribute video can be seen on YouTube.

Just before Covid19 came along and turned the world upside down I used to be a support worker, I loved this job and gave it my all, going out and supporting people is what I enjoyed doing and will miss working with my service users. I had to stop and focus on my son who was having a really bad time with secondary school and matters had got worse where he was discriminated and threatened to the brink of death where I had to get feds involved, not that they were much help. Once Jayden had started to settle into his new school, I decided to start my level 2 in photography. I'm the one you'd always see behind the camera not in front of it. I remember seeing a magical picture of my family, it's very transparent but like it wasn't meant to come out the way it was but looks like a piece of art, I've always wondered if it'd be possible to recreate that picture, I call the magic picture.

I just have always had a love for taking snaps so thought why not take on the course, the course was brilliant I loved it, just being creative with photography, designing my own logo, figuring out how to use photo-shop and designing two posters, one was a Christmas poster, the other was a more in depth as the picture represents an absent father walking away. I had also had great pleasure in creating my own Christmas blog on my YouTube channel, now that gave me such a great buzz.

In my own time I would take my Canon camera everywhere with me, a couple of great picture-perfect moments were taking snaps of my twin nephews and taking snaps at an Asian wedding. The remaining of the course I had completed at home because of covid restrictions but my teacher gave me a great mark and brilliant feedback.

Jamilla

Shaqeal Denise Jayden

Baby Keisha & me

Nanny & me

TENERIFE 2014

Nayel & me

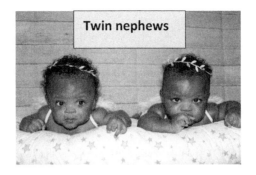

Twin nephews

Jamaica 2016

GCSE Art

Tamira & me clubbing in London

Tamira, me and DAMAGE

Grandad Yahye

Baptism day 2016

Elijah ♡

Walking away photo-shop work

2020/2021

The beginning of 2020 started great as I met Nayel who I love deeply, no matter what anyone says I think everyone is entitled to make their own decisions in life when it comes to relationships. I agree people do care and want to give the best advice, but I am in a courtship with Nayel and we got that good chemistry. He is my go-to and will give it to me straight talking! My ringtone at the moment is a track by Amber Bullock entitled 'I'm so in love with you'.

I hear this and it resonates to my relationship with Ny, the words are spot on when it comes to our relationship and how I feel. He has my heart and has been a great support over the past years to my boys as well as myself. If it's not meant to be only God knows but I feel so positive about this, and our future looks bright. What are the odds our birthdays being a day apart? So, we get to have double the celebrations, we both stubborn heads but we got a great bond. I have never been in a relationship with a man who would quote the bible to me, pray with me over the phone and inspire and uplift my boys to do well in school and the importance of Education.

What more could I ask for? My boys don't have their father to be the guide in their life and to advise them on life's lessons, but I must say Ny has stepped up to that mark and I am thankful for that. In March 2021 my friend Sian, sisters Keisha, Jamilla and I had set ourselves up to raise money for the Sands charity which is the leading stillbirth and neonatal death charity in the UK, this charity is very close to my heart. We did this in memory of my first-born son Elijah. We called ourselves the serenity angels and had got our starter packs which included a sands free tee shirt, a fridge magnet and a tick chart for 50 miles, but we decided to push the boat out that bit further by doing 150 miles for March. My boys Jayden and Shaqeal also took part which made it even more special as they too had the tees to wear.

I remember the first day my boys and I had first stopped off at a local homeless shelter to give a donation of food. We then went onto the canals for a day of treasure hunting which included a lot of walking and doing TikTok videos which had me dancing outdoors in front of passing members of the public, yes, I felt shy, but my boys give me that zing to do what we enjoy and that's being a team and getting out there and making beautiful memories together. Gosh my legs were like jelly come the end of the month, I had only managed to do I think it was 115miles by tracking this on my fitbit which was disappointing to me, but the others aced it, am just glad we managed to raise £85 towards the charity which was our good deed.

November 2020, we sadly lost my nan (moms' side) which was so hard and took its toll

AS GOD IS BY MY SIDE

on the family. It was an honor for me to be allowed to contribute by designing the program booklet and setting out the order of service for my nan's funeral. She had a beautiful sendoff which was on the 23rd of December 2020. I remember both my boys giving their tributes, Jayden had read out a beautiful poem and Shaqeal had sang the song called songbird. This moved me to tears it was so beautiful, my nan would have been so proud of them both and all the tributes that were given that day. My brothers, sisters and I had arranged for doves to be let off at the cemetery but because of bad weather conditions this was sadly unable to happen.

After the passing of my nan, I was so unprepared for what was to come and that was to receive more heartache before the year was through. My boys and I were on a bus ride home from visiting my friend Sian in Dudley when I had got the heart wrenching news that my auntie Joyce (my nan's sister) from Liverpool had passed away, only four weeks after my nan's passing. This was just too much for me to take in. Then that very same day, I hear that my dad's sister auntie Lorna had passed away too. I just cried out in pain, this was just too much to bear it really was, my heart literally just couldn't take anymore. I sobbed my eyes out all the way home. I was just in total shock and complete disbelief of what was happening.

I remember feeling a love loss just like this back in 2012 Christmas day when I heard the news of my nanny passing away. I remember the call from my dad thinking it was a happy Christmas call but no. When he had told me I just screamed out "No!! Please don't tell me this? What happened??" my whole world had come crashing down and my heart was broken. Christmas day was never the same after that, although I do put up the decks and all that, but my heart is not fully in it like it once was. Only five weeks after my nanny passing, we lost our uncle Tony my dad's brother, this was so hard to accept, a big shock to the family we were totally heartbroken beyond words. Grief hits hard like a lightning volt, I always remember my nanny telling me that time is a healer. I believe it's true what she told me, although we never get over the loss because we carry our loved ones in our hearts everyday, but we just learn to live with it.

Two days after Christmas 2020 I contracted covid19 and pneumonia and my health quickly deteriorated. I remember being in my room and crying because I couldn't have that closeness with my boys. The only time I would leave my room was to go toilet, even doing this I would put a mask on and cover my whole face with a scarf because I didn't want to risk my boys getting this from me. Jeeze just taking myself back to this memory as I write this breaks me down in tears because I've never felt so close to death like I did at this point in my life.

I remember my boys leaving food at my door although most of the time I just couldn't stomach eating anything. As the days passed, I would sleep the days away, when I had the strength, I would make my way down to the kitchen and boil up the home remedies of ginger, garlic, black pepper, lemon and honey. My mom and my boy's auntie Janet dropped the ingredients and also, they cooked up food to see us through the coming days.

I was literally living on my home remedies every day, it would be a small relief at times but I still felt ill and started to struggle with my breathing. I had called the ambulance twice and both times they discharged me from home even though they had seen how ill I was. I remember New Year's Eve going downstairs and lying on my settee watching @TheProjectsministry Gospel group on YouTube as they had a live concert. The music was so uplifting and gave me hope, especially the songs called everything, thank you and yours. The lyrics lifted my spirit despite the circumstances, God is good all the time. I slept through the new year and woke up with my health deteriorating, I remember speaking to my mom who had told me I should get to the hospital as soon as possible.

I also called my local GP and explained everything whilst struggling to breathe. My doctor said don't wait around any longer please make your way to the hospital now. In this moment no one would take on my boys because of me having covid19, although I tested positive, and my boys were negative, but I do understand why no one wanted to risk it just in case. Before calling the ambulance, I sat my boys down and told them I'm about to go into hospital, I can call the social services who may take you into a place similar to the movie Annie or you can both stay here at home by yourselves, my boys decided to stay at home. They're quite mature boys for their age so I knew they would be OK.

The ambulance came and had taken me to city hospital where we stayed in the car park for over two hours until a bed became available. I just sat waiting in shivers as my fever kept coming and going and I had on the oxygen mask to help me breathe. Once in the hospital I remember being in some room I had my own cubicle and I was put on a drip, my bloods were taken, there was a lovely Somali nurse her name was Zainab I will never forget her, she seen me crying out "please someone help me" as I struggled to breathe, she gave me oxygen and asked me to turn on my side, I had then fallen asleep once I had become comfortable.

I had woken up as they were taking me upstairs to a ward, I asked where Zainab was and was told she had gone home. My plan is to pass the hospital this year to drop her off a thank you card and a little present because she was so caring and empathetic to how I was. I was so emotionally stressed because of struggling to breathe. I remember being on a ward one night then being moved down to the ICU the next night. My boys, Nayel and my family kept my spirits up with ongoing love, support and prayers.

I will never forget the overwhelming amount of support from across the big pond in the USA from the Onyx family. Rita, her husband Mirth and the kids, I can't thank them enough for the amount of support and love they had shown me and my family whilst I was in my hospital bed, they reached out to us in such a big way, this is something I hold very close to my heart and will never forget such a thoughtful gesture that was shown to me and my family in our time of need. God bless the Onyx family, please do look them up on YouTube they have amazing content.

Once I was settled with my oxygen mask I would WhatsApp video call my boys, Ny and my family to update them on how I was doing. I did fear for my life as I have never in my 38 years experienced something so scary like this. To be discharged and be able to come home to my boys to God be the glory as I have fully recovered. In September 2021 I became a blood donor and donated blood for the first time which is something I have always wanted to do. I am forever grateful God is not through with me yet and I do believe he has a purpose for my LIFE.

THE FUTURE

No one knows what the future holds but I am praying it will be a great one. For the new year I have many goal plans, I wouldn't call it resolutions because they never tend to stick for more than a week. With my goals I plan to start small, one step at a time such as praying often and make more of a commitment to understanding the bible. Over the years the amount of times I've felt like I've drifted 'Backslide' away from my church but never from my faith, no amount of alcohol or clubbing (not that I do go clubbing, grown out of that life) can give such a joy like Jesus does, I am always drawn back to my home the upper room.

This year my boys and I will be back at the gym and swimming with my boys like how we used to do. I want to live healthy and get rid of this weight once and for all, it feels like my only barrier from complete inner happiness is the weight, it's always been a constant battle, but this is a battle that I intend on winning by having self-discipline and accountability. My boys and I would love to go the gym have a good work out swim then head back home, I would absolutely love it and felt so good afterwards. Since my unfortunate fall in the bullring June 2021, it had complicated things as now having a herniated disc in my spine and a damaged nerve in my left leg is quite painful at times and I had become bed ridden and started to comfort eat. The fall had taken me and my boys by surprise, my boys and I were just walking through the bullring and my feet went from under me on what seemed like a huge puddle, I didn't see it coming.

My boys and the security had helped me up and I sat down for a few moments to compose myself and they then took my details. Now coming to think of it, shouldn't it have been me taking their details? Anyway, I was just hoping no one caught it on camera because you know what people are like nowadays, someone's mishap and downfall can be another person's billionaire viewing on YouTube. I am also planning to start the Homeschooling journey for my boys, at one point I never thought I would have taken this route for my boys, but their welfare is my main concern, and I feel this was not considered whilst in mainstream school.

The amount of times I've sent countless emails and had correspondence with the schools and just felt like we were going around in circles, we never really got to the solution for either of my boys and neither one of them were happy with being within the mainstream school setting. Seeing Jayden and the struggles his had to go through at school just takes me back to my childhood and everything I had experienced; it was like de javu all over again. This way with Homeschooling my boys get to have the one to one with a tutor, we can expand on our learning by making it fun and visit many different locations and learn of the history.

To be learning new life skills, as we know that every day we are all learning something new when it comes to education that's for sure. To move out of Birmingham and live somewhere coastal is the dream, I don't think Birmingham is the place to be raising two young black boys to men, especially with how the world is today, kids are killing kids, it is a sign of the end times, and it scares me. My boys don't get involved with the gangs and thugs; they are quite creative young men. I want them to grow in a peaceful place with a beach down the road where they can soak up the sunshine and fresh air. We have lived in this house for 13 years, as we had moved in just a month after my Shaq was born. Over the years we have had nothing but trouble from the neighbours who live in the big house on the corner of our cul de sac close.

The vile abuse that we have endured since being here has been hard, but as the good book says you should turn the other cheek. They have continued to taunt my boys to the point where my boys won't leave the house, it's like we've become prisoners in our own home because of the neighbours from hell. I have reported them to the police before and had to make a report only today because of a load of spit on my front door with a hard sweet stuck on that I had to clean off wearing disposable gloves (not taking any chances with covid19). We really can't wait to get out, God willing that will be this year coming.

To buy my son Elijah a headstone, he did have a wooden cross which was vandalized and broken into pieces, seeing this shattered my heart all over again, I don't know how people can go to cemetery's and cause such vandalism, I did call the police, but nothing was done. I remember speaking with Sands for support, they are amazing. So, I have in mind the headstone I will be getting my baby boy, it's a tatty teddy bear holding a blue blanket and I also plan to plant some roses in the summertime with a little pickard fence.

After completing my level 2 in photography I did apply for university but sadly I was refused because my level 3 in media didn't have enough points? That made no sense to me at all, yes, I was gutted because I had my heart set on starting Uni but as Ny always tells me that when one door closes another one opens and that this wasn't meant for me because God has something else planned for me to do, it won't come in my time but in God's time. I want to become a better version of me, physically and spiritually. I need to focus on living a healthier life and to be that example to my boys. I need to have self-control when it comes to my down days, not to reach out for the tub of vanilla ice-cream with the chocolate powder on top added with the chocolate sauce, not to reach out for the bad stuff, I remember my nan (dad's side) always uses to say what's sweet to the mouth is bitter to the belly and what's bitter to the mouth is sweet to the belly. The naughty things only comfort me for a small amount of time but   is damaging my health in the long run.

I know this, so now I must act upon it and start doing things where I can feel good about myself when am having a down day like going for a walk or doing a dance workout. With the right mindset and determination, I will change my life around, I know I can do it, I just need to overcome the setbacks and blips in the road that happen from time to time. As God is by my side, I will achieve all that I put my heart and soul into. I only have one life to live, I feel like God has given me a second chance to live right and that is exactly what I intend to do.

AS GOD IS BY MY SIDE

SELF-REFLECTION JOURNAL

Writing things down is an effective way of remembering and reflecting on day.

No matter how how little you write, take the time to really think about your day, from time to time you can go back and treasure those memories.

Date: __/__/____ Today I am Grateful For…

_____

_____

_____

What Would Make Today A Great Day?

_____

_____

_____

During the evening just before going to bed take a moment to reflect on your day then List the 3 best things that happened…

1) _____

_____

_____

2) _____

_____

_____

3) _____

_____

_____

Date: __/__/____ Today I am Grateful For…

_____

_____

_____

What Would Make Today A Great Day?

_____

_____

_____

During the evening just before going to bed take a moment to reflect on your day then
List the 3 best things that happened…

1) _____

_____

_____

2) _____

_____

_____

3) _____

_____

_____

Date: __/__/____ Today I am Grateful For...

_____

_____

_____

What Would Make Today A Great Day?

_____

_____

_____

During the evening just before going to bed take a moment to reflect on your day then
List the 3 best things that happened...

1) _____

_____

_____

2) _____

_____

_____

3) _____

_____

_____

Date: __/__/____ Today I am Grateful For…

_____

_____

_____

What Would Make Today A Great Day?

_____

_____

_____

During the evening just before going to bed take a moment to reflect on your day then
List the 3 best things that happened…

1) _____

_____

_____

2) _____

_____

_____

3) _____

_____

_____

Date: __/__/____ Today I am Grateful For...

_____

_____

_____

What Would Make Today A Great Day?

_____

_____

_____

During the evening just before going to bed take a moment to reflect on your day then List the 3 best things that happened...

1) _____

_____

_____

2) _____

_____

_____

3) _____

_____

_____

Date: __/__/____ Today I am Grateful For…

_____

_____

_____

What Would Make Today A Great Day?

_____

_____

_____

During the evening just before going to bed take a moment to reflect on your day then List the 3 best things that happened…

1) _____

_____

_____

2) _____

_____

_____

3) _____

_____

_____

Date: __/__/____ Today I am Grateful For...

_____

_____

_____

What Would Make Today A Great Day?

_____

_____

_____

During the evening just before going to bed take a moment to reflect on your day then List the 3 best things that happened...

1) _____

_____

_____

2) _____

_____

_____

3) _____

_____

_____

Date: __/__/____ Today I am Grateful For…

_____

_____

_____

What Would Make Today A Great Day?

_____

_____

_____

During the evening just before going to bed take a moment to reflect on your day then List the 3 best things that happened…

1) _____

_____

_____

2) _____

_____

_____

3) _____

_____

_____

Date: __/__/____ Today I am Grateful For...

_____

_____

_____

What Would Make Today A Great Day?

_____

_____

_____

During the evening just before going to bed take a moment to reflect on your day then
List the 3 best things that happened...

1) _____

_____

_____

2) _____

_____

_____

3) _____

_____

_____

Date: __/__/____ Today I am Grateful For...

_____

_____

_____

What Would Make Today A Great Day?

_____

_____

_____

During the evening just before going to bed take a moment to reflect on your day then
List the 3 best things that happened...

1) _____

_____

_____

2) _____

_____

_____

3) _____

_____

_____

Date: __/__/____ Today I am Grateful For...

_____

_____

_____

What Would Make Today A Great Day?

_____

_____

_____

During the evening just before going to bed take a moment to reflect on your day then
List the 3 best things that happened...

1) _____

_____

_____

2) _____

_____

_____

3) _____

_____

_____

Date: __/__/____ Today I am Grateful For...

_____

_____

_____

What Would Make Today A Great Day?

_____

_____

_____

During the evening just before going to bed take a moment to reflect on your day then
List the 3 best things that happened...

1) _____

_____

_____

2) _____

_____

_____

3) _____

_____

_____

Date: __/__/____ Today I am Grateful For…

_____

_____

_____

What Would Make Today A Great Day?

_____

_____

_____

During the evening just before going to bed take a moment to reflect on your day then List the 3 best things that happened…

1) _____

_____

_____

2) _____

_____

_____

3) _____

_____

_____

Date: __/__/____ Today I am Grateful For…

_____

_____

_____

What Would Make Today A Great Day?

_____

_____

_____

During the evening just before going to bed take a moment to reflect on your day then
List the 3 best things that happened…

1) _____

_____

_____

2) _____

_____

_____

3) _____

_____

_____

Date: __/__/____ Today I am Grateful For...

_____

_____

_____

What Would Make Today A Great Day?

_____

_____

_____

During the evening just before going to bed take a moment to reflect on your day then
List the 3 best things that happened...

1) _____

_____

_____

2) _____

_____

_____

3) _____

_____

_____

Date: __/__/____ Today I am Grateful For…

_____

_____

_____

What Would Make Today A Great Day?

_____

_____

_____

During the evening just before going to bed take a moment to reflect on your day then
List the 3 best things that happened…

1) _____

_____

_____

2) _____

_____

_____

3) _____

_____

_____

Date: __/__/____ Today I am Grateful For...

_____

_____

_____

What Would Make Today A Great Day?

_____

_____

_____

During the evening just before going to bed take a moment to reflect on your day then List the 3 best things that happened...

1) _____

_____

_____

2) _____

_____

_____

3) _____

_____

_____

Date: __/__/____ Today I am Grateful For…

_____

_____

_____

What Would Make Today A Great Day?

_____

_____

_____

During the evening just before going to bed take a moment to reflect on your day then
List the 3 best things that happened…

1) _____

_____

_____

2) _____

_____

_____

3) _____

_____

_____

Date: __/__/____ Today I am Grateful For...

_____

_____

_____

What Would Make Today A Great Day?

_____

_____

_____

During the evening just before going to bed take a moment to reflect on your day then
List the 3 best things that happened...

1) _____

_____

_____

2) _____

_____

_____

3) _____

_____

_____

Date: __/__/____ Today I am Grateful For...

_____

_____

_____

What Would Make Today A Great Day?

_____

_____

_____

During the evening just before going to bed take a moment to reflect on your day then List the 3 best things that happened...

1) _____

_____

_____

2) _____

_____

_____

3) _____

_____

_____

Date: __/__/____ Today I am Grateful For…

_____

_____

_____

What Would Make Today A Great Day?

_____

_____

_____

During the evening just before going to bed take a moment to reflect on your day then
List the 3 best things that happened…

1) _____

_____

_____

2) _____

_____

_____

3) _____

_____

_____

Date: __/__/____ Today I am Grateful For...

_____

_____

_____

What Would Make Today A Great Day?

_____

_____

_____

During the evening just before going to bed take a moment to reflect on your day then
List the 3 best things that happened...

1) _____

_____

_____

2) _____

_____

_____

3) _____

_____

_____

Date: __/__/____ Today I am Grateful For...

_____

_____

_____

What Would Make Today A Great Day?

_____

_____

_____

During the evening just before going to bed take a moment to reflect on your day then List the 3 best things that happened...

1) _____

_____

_____

2) _____

_____

_____

3) _____

_____

_____

Date: __/__/____ Today I am Grateful For...

_____

_____

_____

What Would Make Today A Great Day?

_____

_____

_____

During the evening just before going to bed take a moment to reflect on your day then
List the 3 best things that happened...

1) _____

_____

_____

2) _____

_____

_____

3) _____

_____

_____

Date: __/__/____ Today I am Grateful For…

_____

_____

_____

What Would Make Today A Great Day?

_____

_____

_____

During the evening just before going to bed take a moment to reflect on your day then
List the 3 best things that happened…

1) _____

_____

_____

2) _____

_____

_____

3) _____

_____

_____

Date: __/__/____ Today I am Grateful For…

_____

_____

_____

What Would Make Today A Great Day?

_____

_____

_____

During the evening just before going to bed take a moment to reflect on your day then List the 3 best things that happened…

1) _____

_____

_____

2) _____

_____

_____

3) _____

_____

_____

Date: __/__/____ Today I am Grateful For...

_____

_____

_____

What Would Make Today A Great Day?

_____

_____

_____

During the evening just before going to bed take a moment to reflect on your day then List the 3 best things that happened...

1) _____

_____

_____

2) _____

_____

_____

3) _____

_____

_____

Date: __/__/____ Today I am Grateful For...

_____

_____

_____

What Would Make Today A Great Day?

_____

_____

_____

During the evening just before going to bed take a moment to reflect on your day then
List the 3 best things that happened...

1) _____

_____

_____

2) _____

_____

_____

3) _____

_____

_____

Date: __/__/____ Today I am Grateful For…

_____

_____

_____

What Would Make Today A Great Day?

_____

_____

_____

During the evening just before going to bed take a moment to reflect on your day then List the 3 best things that happened…

1) _____

_____

_____

2) _____

_____

_____

3) _____

_____

_____

Date: __/__/____ Today I am Grateful For...

_____

_____

_____

What Would Make Today A Great Day?

_____

_____

_____

During the evening just before going to bed take a moment to reflect on your day then List the 3 best things that happened...

1) _____

_____

_____

2) _____

_____

_____

3) _____

_____

_____

Date: __/__/____ Today I am Grateful For...

_____

_____

_____

What Would Make Today A Great Day?

_____

_____

_____

During the evening just before going to bed take a moment to reflect on your day then
List the 3 best things that happened...

1) _____

_____

_____

2) _____

_____

_____

3) _____

_____

_____

Date: __/__/____ Today I am Grateful For…

_____

_____

_____

What Would Make Today A Great Day?

_____

_____

_____

During the evening just before going to bed take a moment to reflect on your day then List the 3 best things that happened…

1) _____

_____

_____

2) _____

_____

_____

3) _____

_____

_____

Date: __/__/____ Today I am Grateful For…

_____

_____

_____

What Would Make Today A Great Day?

_____

_____

_____

During the evening just before going to bed take a moment to reflect on your day then List the 3 best things that happened…

1) _____

_____

_____

2) _____

_____

_____

3) _____

_____

_____

Date: __/__/____ Today I am Grateful For...

_____

_____

_____

What Would Make Today A Great Day?

_____

_____

_____

During the evening just before going to bed take a moment to reflect on your day then List the 3 best things that happened...

1) _____

_____

_____

2) _____

_____

_____

3) _____

_____

_____

Date: __/__/____ Today I am Grateful For...

_____

_____

_____

What Would Make Today A Great Day?

_____

_____

_____

During the evening just before going to bed take a moment to reflect on your day then
List the 3 best things that happened...

1) _____

_____

_____

2) _____

_____

_____

3) _____

_____

_____

Date: __/__/____ Today I am Grateful For…

_____

_____

_____

What Would Make Today A Great Day?

_____

_____

_____

During the evening just before going to bed take a moment to reflect on your day then
List the 3 best things that happened…

1) _____

_____

_____

2) _____

_____

_____

3) _____

_____

_____

Date: __/__/____ Today I am Grateful For…

_____

_____

_____

What Would Make Today A Great Day?

_____

_____

_____

During the evening just before going to bed take a moment to reflect on your day then List the 3 best things that happened…

1) _____

_____

_____

2) _____

_____

_____

3) _____

_____

_____

Date: __/__/____ Today I am Grateful For...

_____

_____

_____

What Would Make Today A Great Day?

_____

_____

_____

During the evening just before going to bed take a moment to reflect on your day then
List the 3 best things that happened...

1) _____

_____

_____

2) _____

_____

_____

3) _____

_____

_____

Date: __/__/____ Today I am Grateful For...

_____

_____

_____

What Would Make Today A Great Day?

_____

_____

_____

During the evening just before going to bed take a moment to reflect on your day then
List the 3 best things that happened...

1) _____

_____

_____

2) _____

_____

_____

3) _____

_____

_____

Date: __/__/____ Today I am Grateful For…

_____

_____

_____

What Would Make Today A Great Day?

_____

_____

_____

During the evening just before going to bed take a moment to reflect on your day then List the 3 best things that happened…

1) _____

_____

_____

2) _____

_____

_____

3) _____

_____

_____

Date: __/__/____ Today I am Grateful For…

_____

_____

_____

What Would Make Today A Great Day?

_____

_____

_____

During the evening just before going to bed take a moment to reflect on your day then List the 3 best things that happened…

1) _____

_____

_____

2) _____

_____

_____

3) _____

_____

_____

Date: __/__/____ Today I am Grateful For...

_____

_____

_____

What Would Make Today A Great Day?

_____

_____

_____

During the evening just before going to bed take a moment to reflect on your day then List the 3 best things that happened...

1) _____

_____

_____

2) _____

_____

_____

3) _____

_____

_____

Date: __/__/____ Today I am Grateful For…

_____

_____

_____

What Would Make Today A Great Day?

_____

_____

_____

During the evening just before going to bed take a moment to reflect on your day then
List the 3 best things that happened…

1) _____

_____

_____

2) _____

_____

_____

3) _____

_____

_____

Date: __/__/____ Today I am Grateful For...

_____

_____

_____

What Would Make Today A Great Day?

_____

_____

_____

During the evening just before going to bed take a moment to reflect on your day then
List the 3 best things that happened...

1) _____

_____

_____

2) _____

_____

_____

3) _____

_____

_____

Date: __/__/____ Today I am Grateful For…

_____

_____

_____

What Would Make Today A Great Day?

_____

_____

_____

During the evening just before going to bed take a moment to reflect on your day then
List the 3 best things that happened…

1) _____

_____

_____

2) _____

_____

_____

3) _____

_____

_____

Date: __/__/____ Today I am Grateful For…

_____

_____

_____

What Would Make Today A Great Day?

_____

_____

_____

During the evening just before going to bed take a moment to reflect on your day then
List the 3 best things that happened…

1) _____

_____

_____

2) _____

_____

_____

3) _____

_____

_____

Date: __/__/____ Today I am Grateful For…

_____

_____

_____

What Would Make Today A Great Day?

_____

_____

_____

During the evening just before going to bed take a moment to reflect on your day then List the 3 best things that happened…

1) _____

_____

_____

2) _____

_____

_____

3) _____

_____

_____

Date: __/__/____ Today I am Grateful For…

_____

_____

_____

What Would Make Today A Great Day?

_____

_____

_____

During the evening just before going to bed take a moment to reflect on your day then List the 3 best things that happened…

1) _____

_____

_____

2) _____

_____

_____

3) _____

_____

_____

Date: __/__/____ Today I am Grateful For...

_____

_____

_____

What Would Make Today A Great Day?

_____

_____

_____

During the evening just before going to bed take a moment to reflect on your day then
List the 3 best things that happened...

1) _____

_____

_____

2) _____

_____

_____

3) _____

_____

_____

Date: __/__/____ Today I am Grateful For…

_____

_____

_____

What Would Make Today A Great Day?

_____

_____

_____

During the evening just before going to bed take a moment to reflect on your day then
List the 3 best things that happened…

1) _____

_____

_____

2) _____

_____

_____

3) _____

_____

_____

Date: __/__/_____ Today I am Grateful For…

_____

_____

_____

What Would Make Today A Great Day?

_____

_____

_____

During the evening just before going to bed take a moment to reflect on your day then List the 3 best things that happened…

1) _____

_____

_____

2) _____

_____

_____

3) _____

_____

_____

Date: __/__/____ Today I am Grateful For...

_____

_____

_____

What Would Make Today A Great Day?

_____

_____

_____

During the evening just before going to bed take a moment to reflect on your day then List the 3 best things that happened...

1) _____

_____

_____

2) _____

_____

_____

3) _____

_____

_____

Date: __/__/____ Today I am Grateful For…

_____

_____

_____

What Would Make Today A Great Day?

_____

_____

_____

During the evening just before going to bed take a moment to reflect on your day then
List the 3 best things that happened…

1) _____

_____

_____

2) _____

_____

_____

3) _____

_____

_____

Date: __/__/____ Today I am Grateful For…

_____

_____

_____

What Would Make Today A Great Day?

_____

_____

_____

During the evening just before going to bed take a moment to reflect on your day then List the 3 best things that happened…

1) _____

_____

_____

2) _____

_____

_____

3) _____

_____

_____

Date: __/__/____ Today I am Grateful For…

_____

_____

_____

What Would Make Today A Great Day?

_____

_____

_____

During the evening just before going to bed take a moment to reflect on your day then
List the 3 best things that happened…

1) _____

_____

_____

2) _____

_____

_____

3) _____

_____

_____

Date: __/__/____ Today I am Grateful For...

_____

_____

_____

What Would Make Today A Great Day?

_____

_____

_____

During the evening just before going to bed take a moment to reflect on your day then
List the 3 best things that happened...

1) _____

_____

_____

2) _____

_____

_____

3) _____

_____

_____

Date: __/__/____ Today I am Grateful For...

_____

_____

_____

What Would Make Today A Great Day?

_____

_____

_____

During the evening just before going to bed take a moment to reflect on your day then
List the 3 best things that happened...

1) _____

_____

_____

2) _____

_____

_____

3) _____

_____

_____

Date: __/__/____ Today I am Grateful For...

_____

_____

_____

What Would Make Today A Great Day?

_____

_____

_____

During the evening just before going to bed take a moment to reflect on your day then List the 3 best things that happened...

1) _____

_____

_____

2) _____

_____

_____

3) _____

_____

_____

ABOUT THE AUTHOR

Brummie born mom of two boys Chantelle also known as Chantastic83 gives you an insight to her personal life. How her faith in God has kept her through some real hard times. Here she shares her downs as well as her most empowering moments on this journey we call life, how she made it work as a single parent and her plans for the future ahead. As God is by my side is the debut memoir by Chantelle Stephens.

I CAN DO ALL THINGS THROUGH CHRIST WHO STRENGTHENS ME
Philippians 4:13

Wait on the lord and be of good courage psalm 27:14

AWARENESS

It is very important to me to raise awareness. I have felt at my lowest where I thought there was no way out and at that time, I had no one to talk to and take my hand to let me know that everything was going to be ok, but my faith in God kept me. Mental health in children needs awareness! And is a serious matter. If I could tell the 12-year-old me anything it would be to speak out, don't suffer in silence, there is support for you and you're not alone. Children need to be acknowledged and supported. Parents if you notice a change in behaviour with your child such as depression or anxiety there are support networks out there that you can reach out to for support.

Forward Thinking Birmingham **0300 300 0099**
Pause Birmingham

Childline **0800 1111**

Kooth.com
Papyrus-org.uk

HOPELINE UK **0800 068 4141**

YoungMinds.org.uk **0808 802 5544** (parents' helpline)

National suicide prevention line **0800 689 5652**

Every day in the UK, 13 babies are stillborn or die shortly after birth. The charity Sands works to save babies' lives and support anyone affected by pregnancy loss or the death of a baby. If you or someone you know needs support, Sands is here for you.

Sands Bereavement Support Team are available on **0808 164 3332** 10am to 3pm Monday to Friday and 6-9pm Tuesday and Thursday evenings. You can also email helpline@sands.org.uk for support. www.sands.org.uk/support

Printed in Great Britain
by Amazon